—— Imagine Living Here ——

This Place Is COLD

Vicki Cobb

illustrated by
Barbara Lavallee

WALKER BOOKS FOR YOUNG READERS
AN IMPRINT OF BLOOMSBURY
NEW YORK   LONDON   NEW DELHI   SYDNEY

P9-DIJ-343

Wilsonville Public Library

For Carol and Vic Hussey

The author gratefully acknowledges the assistance
of the following Alaskans: Jan Westfall, Dee McKenna, Roz Goodman,
Jane Behlke, and Jim and Emma Walton.

✳

Author's Note

There are many distinct groups of Native people in Alaska, including Inuit
and Yup'ik peoples. I have chosen to use the word "Eskimo" throughout this
book because it is the one term that encompasses all these cultures. (In Canada,
where the population is less diverse, they prefer to be called Inuit.)

Original text copyright © 1989 by Vicki Cobb
Updated text copyright © 2013 by Vicki Cobb
Illustrations copyright © 1989 by Barbara Lavallee

All rights reserved. No part of this book may be reproduced or transmitted in any form
or by any means, electronic or mechanical, including photocopying, recording, or by any information storage and
retrieval system, without permission in writing from the publisher.

First published in the United States of America in 1989; revised edition published in January 2013
by Walker Books for Young Readers, an imprint of Bloomsbury Publishing, Inc.
www.bloomsburykids.com

For information about permission to reproduce selections from this book, write to
Permissions, Walker BFYR, 175 Fifth Avenue, New York, New York 10010

The Library of Congress has cataloged the original edition as follows:
Cobb, Vicki.
This place is cold / by Vicki Cobb ; illustrated by Barbara Lavallee.
p.   cm.—(Imagine living here)
Summary: Focuses on the land, animals, plants, and climate of Alaska, presenting it as an example of a place
where it is so cold your hair can freeze and break off.
ISBN 0-8027-6852-0 (hardcover) • ISBN 0-8027-6853-9 (reinforced)
ISBN 0-8027-7340-0 (paperback)
1. Alaska—Description and travel—1981—Juvenile literature. 2. Cold regions—Juvenile literature. [1. Alaska—
Description and travel. 2. Cold regions.] I. Lavallee, Barbara, ill. II. Title. III. Series: Cobb, Vicki. Imagine living here.
F910.5.C63 1989   917.98—dc19   88-25919   CIP   AC

ISBN 978-0-8027-3401-3 (revised)

Art created with transparent watercolor painted on 300 lb Fabriano cold pressed watercolor paper
Typeset in Amasis Std
Book design by Regina Roff

Printed in China by C&C Offset Printing Co., Ltd., Shenzhen, Guangdong
1 3 5 7 9 10 8 6 4 2

All papers used by Bloomsbury Publishing, Inc., are natural, recyclable products
made from wood grown in well-managed forests. The manufacturing processes
conform to the environmental regulations of the country of origin.

How Cold Is It?

If you visited Alaska during the winter, the first things you would notice are the cold and the darkness. How cold can it get? Temperatures can drop 50 degrees below zero Fahrenheit (45.6 degrees below zero Celsius)—and even lower. People plug their cars into electrical outlets in their garages so that the special engine heaters can keep the batteries from getting too cold to start. Firewood is so frozen that one tap of an ax shatters a log. Snow squeaks loudly when you step on it. Sometimes the wind is so strong you have to walk at a slant. Your breath turns instantly into tiny ice crystals that glitter in the sun. Your eyebrows and eyelashes freeze, but you don't dare rub them for fear they will break off.

Why Is It So Cold?

In the winter, the North Pole points away from the sun. So the top of the world, called the Arctic Circle, is always in darkness. Just below the Arctic Circle, the sun comes up around lunchtime for only a few hours. Children wake up when it's dark, go to school in the dark, and come home in the dark. If there is almost no sunlight, it gets cold.

On some winter nights, the sky is decorated by an incredible display of swirling colored curtains of light called the *aurora borealis*, or northern lights.

Rivers of Ice

Millions of years ago, rivers of ice, called *glaciers*, began to form in valleys all over Alaska. Snow piles up from year to year and since it is always cold, it doesn't melt. The weight of the piled snow changes the snow into ice. Then the ice is packed so hard that it changes color from ice-cube clear to a bright blue-green.

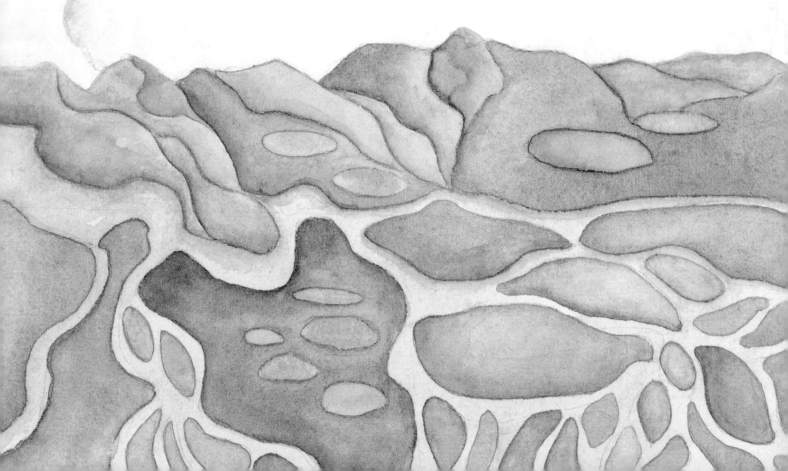

Glaciers are nature's giant bulldozers. The heavy, old ice starts moving very slowly down the mountain, carrying along rocks that grind up the soil. After millions of years, glaciers carve valleys that were V-shaped into U-shaped ones. In some places, the land looks as if a giant melon scoop has been at work.

When some glaciers reach the sea or lakes, pieces break off into chunks of floating ice called *icebergs*. Other glaciers just melt, leaving behind long, high hills of dirt. The melting glacial waters form many curved streams called "braided" rivers.

Frozen Ground

In some places the ground is permanently frozen. This kind of land is called *permafrost*. Here and there, deep in the permafrost soil, are blocks of ice called *ice lenses*. When a house is built over permafrost or an ice lens, the heat from the house may cause melting. The water seeps away and the thawed ground sinks. The part of the house that rests on the thawed ground will sink too. Sometimes to straighten out a house, people use jacks, like the ones you use to change tires, only stronger.

In many places, the permafrost is covered with a thick layer of short, scrubby plants, like berry bushes. This land is called the *tundra*, which comes from a Russian word meaning "bare hill." The heat from the sun is trapped by the plants and doesn't pass into the soil. So the tundra plants stop the permafrost from melting.

How Do Some Plants Survive the Cold?

The plants that grow on the tundra must be able to survive the extreme cold and dryness. There are no large trees here because even in the summer when the ground thaws a little, there isn't enough water for them to grow.

*Lichen*s (LI-kens) are the survival champions of the tundra. They have thrived for millions of years because they are a unique partnership of two plants. One part is a *fungus*, which cannot make its own food but is shaped to catch rainwater. The other part is made up of millions of microscopic green plants called *algae* (AL-gee), which use the water collected by the fungus to make food. Lichens can grow on rocks since they have no roots and don't need soil. But they grow very, very slowly. A 2-inch (5-centimeter)-wide lichen may be hundreds of years old.

Tiny Plants That Feed Large Herds

These tiny plants attract reindeer and their slightly larger cousins, the caribou, to the tundra to graze on lichens all summer. The tundra is also the home of the largest member of the deer family, the moose. Males, called bulls, can be 7.5 feet (2.3 meters) tall at the shoulders and weigh almost a ton (907.2 kilograms). Their antlers alone can weigh 100 pounds (45.4 kg). Bulls shed their antlers and grow a new set every year, which they use to fight over the females, called cows.

Shaggy Survivors

The musk ox has survived unchanged for millions of years, in part by eating plants of the tundra. It gets its name from the sharp, sweet "musky" smell that the males give off. When danger threatens, musk-oxen herds form a circle with their young in the center. This protects the young from wolves and other predators. But they are no match for human guns and arrows. A hundred years ago they were hunted almost to extinction for their meat and their wool.

The musk ox has a long, shaggy coat that sways like a skirt in the breeze. Next to the body is a thick layer of wool that is eight times warmer than sheep wool and softer than cashmere. This wool is shed in patches in the summer. Eskimo women gather it and can comb tame musk oxen to collect more. They knit this fine wool into very expensive hats and scarves. Laws protecting the musk ox have helped this animal make a remarkable recovery. Today, musk oxen are raised for their wool on ranches and some have been set free to roam the tundra again in wild herds.

Why Do Bears Thrive in the Cold?

The most dangerous animals in Alaska are the bears. The brown bear, the world's largest meat eater, weighs a powerful 1,600 pounds (725.7 kg)—almost a ton. But no one wants to run into a hungry grizzly or polar bear either. All bears kill small animals for food, and some will attack a sleeping camper and raid a tent for food.

People who travel in bear territory learn to respect bears. Some hikers use a walking stick with bells that ring with each step so they won't surprise the bears. And campers should never eat near their tents, because bears might be drawn to the smell of food and surprise them while they're sleeping.

In addition to eating meat and fish, bears have a sweet tooth and love berries and honey. They must load on enough weight throughout the summer and fall to survive through the coldest winter months as they sleep snugly in their dens.

An Unusual Winter Coat

A white polar bear has fur that is different from all other animals. Close to the body is a thick layer of woolly fur for warmth. Long, clear *guard hairs*, which are hollow like plastic straws, stick out to keep the fur from getting matted down when the polar bear swims in icy water. Water is easily shaken off this stiff outer coat.

Staying Warm for the Hunt

A polar bear's white coat is protective camouflage in the ice and snow. But white reflects sunlight and its needed heat. Black is the color that absorbs warmth, so nature gave polar bears black skin. The clear guard hairs trap the sun's heat rays and conduct them down to the skin, making it warm. Under the skin is a layer of fat that stores this heat to keep the bear warmer longer. Polar bears also have thick fur between the pads on the bottoms of their feet to keep their feet from freezing as they walk for miles (kilometers) over the frigid ice.

Polar bears are skilled hunters and fishers. They eat sea mammals like small whales and walruses. But their favorite food is the seal. It takes a lot of skill for a polar bear to catch a seal. There's no way the bear can outswim a seal to catch it. So they search for seals resting on the ice or wait at the edge of the ice, then attack when seals come up for air.

What Is the Worst Threat to Sea Mammals?

Polar bears are not the worst enemy of sea mammals. People have hunted them for centuries. Seals have been hunted for their shiny, thick fur. Walruses have been hunted for their ivory tusks, which they use to dig up clams and mollusks on the bottom of the sea. Unluckily for the walrus, the ivory can be carved into tools, jewelry, and small statues. Today, to protect the walrus and other sea mammals, only Eskimos are allowed to hunt them and carve the ivory.

All sea mammals have a layer of blubber under their skin to keep them warm. Eskimos hunt sea mammals for their blubber as well as for their meat. Eating animal fat helps the Eskimos form a layer of fat under their own skins to stay warm. Whales, the largest mammals of all, have the most blubber. And they were almost hunted to extinction for it. That whale blubber was cooked down into fine oil that people once used in lamps to light their homes and in factories to fuel the industrial revolution.

The Whale with the Strainer in Its Mouth

Instead of teeth, a *baleen whale* has a mouth full of baleen—long, flexible plates with fringes trailing behind. It eats by swimming along with its mouth open, straining large amounts of water filled with millions of tiny plants and animals called *plankton*, which float in the ocean. Some baleen whales eat up to 4.5 tons (4,082 kg) of this stuff a day!

Before plastic was invented, baleen was used to make umbrella ribs, eyeglass frames, and the stiff supports of ladies' underwear. Baleen can also be peeled into long thin strips and woven into beautiful baskets.

An Extraordinary Journey

There are many different kinds of fish in Alaskan seas and rivers. But the most popular and amazing is the salmon.

Salmon eggs hatch in freshwater streams known as *spawning grounds*. Baby salmon live in their spawning grounds until they are two years old. Then they travel downstream. The streams get larger and become rivers until finally they join the ocean, where the salmon spend their adult life. When a red salmon is about four years old, it is ready to lay eggs. So it begins an incredible return journey back to the exact place where it hatched. This means traveling upstream for hundreds of miles (hundreds of kilometers), swimming against the current, leaping over waterfalls, in an exhausting trip to its spawning grounds. The females lay their eggs, the males fertilize them, and then the adults die.

Bears and fishermen know that the best way to fish for salmon is to catch them as they make their last journey upriver. Bears eat most of what they catch. But people can be greedy and overfish. Today there are laws that control who may fish for salmon and how many fish they can take, to make sure there will be plenty of salmon in the future.

What Kind of People Live in Alaska?

The first people to settle Alaska were Native Americans and Eskimos. They were expert hunters and fishermen. They traveled over the snow with sleds drawn by teams of dogs. They made boats and clothing from animal skins and bones. They told stories, made up songs, and created art that showed how they lived and how they felt about their lives.

Why would other people come to this harsh land? The first outsiders came to profit from the plentiful wildlife. Whalers wanted oil and baleen. Trappers wanted the thick, shiny furs of seals, otters, beavers, arctic foxes, and wolves to sell for high prices in the world of fashion. Fishermen wanted the millions of salmon in the rivers.

Around the beginning of the twentieth century, gold was discovered in the Klondike and on the beaches of the Bering Sea. Thousands of hopeful gold miners rushed to Alaska. The people who sold them supplies were not far behind. Besides gold, a giant copper mine promised wealth. Some of the people got rich, but most didn't. Still, many of them stayed. They married, had children, and made new lives in Alaska's small villages.

How Did Outsiders Change Alaska?

All these new people needed ways to get around. A railroad was built to connect the main cities of Anchorage and Fairbanks. But there were many people who lived in remote places, called the *bush*, that you could reach only by dogsled, snowmobile, boat (after the ice melts), or airplane. Villages in the bush, like Unalakleet and Shaktoolik, created an opportunity for a new kind of work, the bush pilot. Bush pilots are skilled in taking off and landing planes on dirt runways or on frozen lakes. They bring food, medicine, mail, and contact with the outside world.

It's no big deal to have a pilot's license in Alaska. One person in every sixty-one has a license. There are more private planes per person there than in any other part of the world. Alaskans think of their planes as you might think of a family car. People use them to go to vacation cabins, to visit friends in bush villages, and to get to a major airport to catch a jet to the rest of the world.

Black Gold

In 1969, a "supergiant" oil field was discovered in the Arctic Circle. Oil has been called "black gold" because the modern world depends on it for so many things. The problem with the Arctic oil was how to get it to the rest of the world. There were no highways or railroads, and the nearby sea was frozen for nine months of the year. The only solution was to build a pipeline 800 miles (1,287.5 km) long to pump the oil to an ice-free port where supertankers could load it.

Eight oil companies got together and spent eight billion dollars to build the pipeline. The work was hard and uncomfortable. Workers spent long hours in the cold, lonely wilderness. But it paid well—very well. So thousands of young people came from all over America and the rest of the world. Each worker wore three layers of clothing under a down parka and overalls, two layers of gloves, three pairs of socks, a hat under a hardhat, and a face scarf. It took ten years and more than seventy thousand men and women to build a pipeline that is one of the wonders of modern engineering.

Endless Summer Days

Summer in the far north is just the opposite of the winter. The North Pole points toward the sun, and the Arctic Circle is always in sunlight. Inside the Arctic Circle, the sun doesn't set from March 21 to September 21. About 400 miles (643.7 km) below the Arctic Circle, the sun shines almost all night long. This constant sun enables farmers to grow crops like cabbage and potatoes, even though summer is short. There is even enough daylight for a farmer to have once grown a cabbage that weighed 120 pounds (54.4 kg)!

All this daylight changes the way people act. You need dark window shades to make it feel like bedtime. Children feel like playing all night long. In spite of all the sunlight, the summers near the Arctic Circle are not very warm, although sunny summer days feel warm to the people used to living there. Children in Alaska begin wearing shorts to school when the temperature is about 50 degrees Fahrenheit (10 degrees C). In a few places, like Fairbanks, summer temperatures may go as high as 85 or 90 degrees Fahrenheit (29.4 or 32.2 degrees C).

Is Alaska Heating Up?

Global warming has raised the average temperature 3.5 degrees Fahrenheit (1.9 degrees C) in the past thirty years, more than anyplace else on Earth. Polar ice is melting, glaciers are retreating, and there are more storms and forest fires. The permafrost is thawing, causing problems with roads and the oil pipeline. Animal habitats are disappearing. The melting ice cap threatens the polar bears, a warning of coming dangers to other arctic animals. Yet most of Alaska is still wilderness—a frontier for those with an adventuresome spirit.

For some, life in Alaska is a test of themselves. Global warming is bringing a new set of challenges. This is a place of opportunity for doers. Can you imagine living here?